transforming
your**workplace**

ADRYAN BELL

INSTITUTE OF PERSONNEL AND DEVELOPMENT

Sketches and illustrations: Gillian Stewart

First published in 2000

Design by Curve
Typesetting by Paperweight
Printed in Great Britain by
The Guernsey Press, Channel Islands

British Library Cataloguing in Publication Data
A catalogue record for this book is available from the
British Library

ISBN
0-85292-856-4

The views expressed in this book are the author's own and
may not necessarily reflect those of the IPD.

**INSTITUTE OF PERSONNEL
AND DEVELOPMENT**

IPD House, Camp Road, London SW19 4UX
Tel.: 020-8971 9000   Fax: 020-8263 3333
Registered office as above. Registered Charity No. 1038333.
A company limited by guarantee. Registered in England No. 2931892.

contents

Other titles in the series:

beginnings

My first experience of an office workplace was some 20 years ago, when I was working in the Unemployment Benefit Service at the height of an unemployment boom. A lot of staff were taken on at that time, and I had to share one corner of a desk with three other people. Luckily, there was always somewhere to work, because staff were frequently off sick. Looking back, I wonder to what extent that physical workplace contributed to sickness. It certainly didn't make the job easier.

As my career progressed, I used many different offices, in both the public and private sectors – but none of them was really any better. Apparently designed for a previous era, they did not recognise the needs of the time – or the advances that we have seen in recent years in technology, working practices and attitudes to work.

Finally, just a few years ago I was involved in the award-winning 'Workplace of the Future' project for the government agency Scottish Enterprise – during which a very traditional workplace was transformed into a futuristic and dynamic working environment where people *wanted* to be. In the course of the project I discovered the positive influence that an appropriate, well-designed working environment can have on people and the way they work. This is what I call the *workplace opportunity*.

This book aims to share that discovery with you, whatever your role in the office may be. The workplace opportunity is there for everyone to take – and the rewards are both wide-ranging and substantial. Best of all, the secrets to success are simpler than you may think. Now read on...

the changing office 1

Understanding the trends and opportunities

The pressure to re-examine the role of the office environment in supporting business and organisational aspirations has never been stronger. And not without good reason. Let's first look back at where we have come from.

Look around you

You may be in an old or a new office. You may consider that it helps you to work better; you may not. But it does have a particular layout and style that have probably developed over time through a range of influences, not all of them necessarily logical or even linked to day-to-day business. There will, undoubtedly, be some scope for change, and for improved efficiency and effectiveness.

> Put yourself in the shoes of a complete stranger to your working environment. What would it tell that person about your organisation – about what it does and how it does it?

Workplace change can sometimes be very complicated, however. It requires a number of qualities to be successful, not least among them vision, imagination, determination and diplomacy. It also requires simplicity and common sense which, for some strange reason, have not always featured strongly in office design.

But the qualities mentioned are ones that we all possess, to a greater or lesser extent. We use them all the time, in all aspects of our lives. What we need to do is to apply them to our workplace. Quite simply, we should look at our workplace in a completely different light.

Yesterday's workplace

Office workplaces are hardly a new thing! They have been around in something like their present form for over 100 years. And most of us will have had some experience of them: well over half of the UK workforce is to be found in offices.

Long before the age of computers, the earliest offices were predominantly about processing information on paper; there was little need for people to interact. Such places were in effect 'clerical factories', in which the desk and the chair provided all the physical elements needed for employees to carry out tasks. A strong sense of supervision prevailed, which, as a result, led to a style and allocation of workspace that clearly expressed the office hierarchy.

New influences

The introduction and continuing advances of *information and communications technology* have, of course, revolutionised the way business is undertaken – the very nature of office work has changed. Routine-process work has (for many) greatly diminished, freeing employees to add value in more dynamic and creative ways.

Interaction and the exchange of information and knowledge are now key components that need to be supported in today's working environment. Employees are much more empowered about how, and even where and when, they do their jobs.

But the office does not exist in isolation: changing attitudes in society at large are also influencing the increase in informality and flexibility of working practices – often referred to as *new ways of working*.

All these developments I regard as the *workplace dynamics*. However, despite such developments, most office workplaces are nonetheless still strongly based (in terms of style and layout) on the needs of those early 'clerical factories'. This is true not just of old buildings, but of brand new ones too.

Does your office reflect modern workplace dynamics?

Does it truly support and reflect the diversity of modern office work?

The diversity of office work

Studies of the way office workspace is used can be extremely revealing. A typical study would involve regularly checking desks or other workspaces (such as meeting areas) every hour – or even every half hour – for two or three weeks. This allows a reasonably realistic sample of office life to be captured. The study would not just note whether the workspace is used or empty, but also exactly what type of activity is being performed there.

A simple study typically shows that:

● workspace is heavily underused – reflecting the *dynamics* of office work (meetings, informal interaction, working away from the office and so on)

■ a wide range of activities – often conflicting or combined – are undertaken, reflecting the *diversity* of office work (reading, typing, writing, PC work, telephone calls, meetings, reflection and so on).

All workspace costs money, so empty space is a drain on finances. Employees' time (obviously) costs money too, so inappropriate or ineffective worksettings can also be a financial drain.

As the graph on page 7 indicates, workspace can often be empty or unused for around 50 per cent of the working day. For some teams this percentage may be even higher. Such a

Typical Time Utilisation Study© of workspace © DEGW

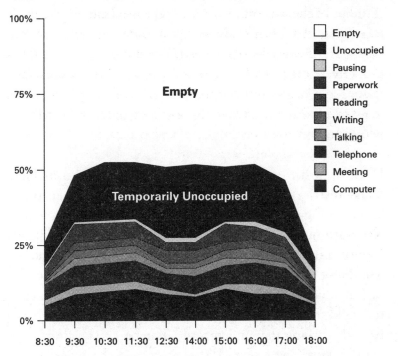

finding should be interpreted with care, but it does provide a thought-provoking pointer towards opportunities for change and improvement.

> Try undertaking such a study of the use of workspace as a sample or initial exercise, just to see what it tells you about the use and suitability of *your* workplace.

Analyse your own workspace

A simple do-it-yourself exercise can be extremely useful. It is unlikely that your findings will differ too much from the typical trends outlined. But you do need to set up such studies properly, not least to ensure that the motives for undertaking them are properly understood by staff: make clear that it is the use of space, and not the work of individuals, that is being studied.

Draw up a list of all the workspaces you want to include. Don't restrict yourself to just desks and offices – corridors and meeting spaces are also important. Then plan a logical route around all the workspaces and list them accordingly. Devise a table based on this list that allows you to record whether the space is in use or not, as well as the sort of activity undertaken there. You can then arrange for someone to 'walk' the route on a regular basis during the course of a typical working day and record what he or she finds. It is actually possible for up to 150 workspaces to be covered once an hour!

You can get specialists to assist you with your study, particularly where large numbers of spaces are involved. They may use special hand-held recording devices to speed up the recording process. Such specialists will also, importantly, have experience in how best to analyse and interpret the data you collect, and add some 'independent' credibility to the conclusions of the study.

Workplace culture

Many offices have developed around the extremes of either open-plan or cellular offices, usually organised according to status and tradition rather than practical need. Why else is it, for example, that the chairman of a company – who may be in only two days a month – gets such a big office?

This is generally all acknowledged as part of an organisation's culture or, as it is often described, *the way we do things around here*. Organisational culture is a fundamental consideration in workplace transformation – we shall be exploring this in more detail later.

But although the extremes of open or cellular workspaces have their role, they are often the wrong environment for those that work in them. It is unlikely, for example, that an open-plan desk is the perfect setting for meetings, confidential telephone work or work requiring unbroken concentration; it may instead be fine for routine telephone, PC or paper-based work. Similarly, is the interactive, knowledge-sharing executive at best advantage when hidden in an enclosed office?

In between the extremes are some much more appropriate and interesting workplace models that can provide a better match for the diversity and dynamics of office work. We shall be looking at some examples in Chapter 2.

Adaptability

An important part of workplace dynamics is the need for offices to respond to ongoing business and organisational change – and this often involves change that can't be predicted or controlled.

One of the problems with a workplace based upon organisational structure, ownership and status is that it has to be changed every time a new team is formed, or even when someone gets promoted. We move desks, knock down walls and shuffle people round, but it is important to be aware that, in doing so, we don't fundamentally change anything. We call this phenomenon *churn*. And it costs money – a lot more than many people realise. Churn is also a big disturbance to business operations. So we need to find better ways of making the workplace adaptable without the need for continual churn.

How many times has your workplace been moved or adjusted in recent years?

Did anything really change in terms of the effectiveness and appropriateness of that workplace?

New role of the workplace

Organisations are now realising that, along with new technology, the physical workplace is one of the most significant tools to support staff in business effectiveness. Two things in particular are clear:

- Get the workplace right, and it can work wonders.

- Get it wrong, and it can stifle business activities and hinder development and progress.

And getting it wrong can also be a consequence of doing nothing.

It is worth noting that, despite increasing flexibility in working practices (eg in home- and remote working), the office workplace is still very much at the heart of most organisations. It may be used at present in different ways; it may even in the future be smaller. But one thing is sure: it will continue to play a vital role in the life of an organisation and its people.

Increasingly, the workplace will be used for specific reasons, not just out of habit or routine. It will be used as one of a number of working options, and be the place where people go, in particular, to interact and obtain and exchange information and knowledge. These functions will be an increasingly important and valuable aspect of people's jobs. But to fulfil this new role effectively, many workplaces will need to evolve significantly.

A catalyst for change

The office workplace is much more than just a provider of functionality. As a physical thing that people can see, feel and touch, it can have an amazing psychological effect on people – both in a positive and a negative sense.

It can affect the mood, creativity and motivation of staff. It can provide a corporate image that stimulates and impresses customers and visitors. It can also, if wrong, detrimentally affect staff morale, productivity and customer perceptions. In other words, it has the potential to be a powerful influence on all aspects of business.

For this reason the workplace can be the perfect catalyst for change, improvement and progression – at a team, departmental or organisational level. And indeed workplace change is increasingly being used in this important way by organisations. A director at Scottish Enterprise once said that the significant cultural and business changes that his team had made in the first 10 months in their new workspace would have probably taken 10 years had they remained in their old environment.

The bigger picture

The planning and design of workspace cannot be undertaken in isolation from the needs of the people who work there and the work that they perform. You need to consider the whole picture of *people*, *process* and *place*, and how all these aspects interact and overlap (as shown in the graphic opposite).

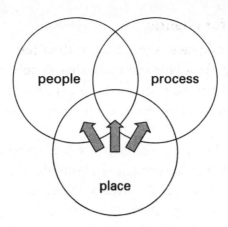

Similarly, it is also not sensible or logical for an organisation to change and develop its people or its business processes without considering the workplace. Yet so often this happens.

new concepts   2

An explanation of new workplace models, options and choices

Chapter 1 has provided some useful context and reasoning behind the need to consider transforming your workplace. But *what* needs to be different? Before rushing into making changes, it is worth exploring some of the options.

The increase in office dynamism and diversity that we saw in Chapter 1 points toward the need for a wider range of worksettings to match the way in which people actually work. There is also a need for increased effectiveness, adaptability, sharing and comfort in the workplace – and even perhaps some excitement! This implies a decisive move away from the 'clerical factory', where staff are simply slotted in somewhere with a desk and a chair, irrespective of the nature of their work.

Menu of options

Providing a more suitable balance of worksettings is a simple but vital element in effectively transforming a workplace.

There are many interesting worksetting options available; they should be viewed as essentially a menu from which you may select the best configuration to match your organisational needs. Some of these options are listed below, with illustrations.

Worksetting options

Here are some descriptions and graphics of traditional and 'alternative' settings to mix and match for your needs.

Owned desk

An owned desk is a dedicated 'homebase' for staff working in the office at a desk most of the time – ideally, allocated on the basis of business (ie functional) need, not according to status.

Owned office

This is an enclosed 'homebase' for staff working in-house most of the time and regularly in need of the facilities provided by such an office (eg privacy, confidentiality and concentration).

Shared (hot) desk

A shared or hot desk is used by staff requiring it for only part of their time because they are often at meetings or away from the office. It can be used to mix and encourage communication among staff, and can also be arranged in 'zones' to keep teams together and provide identity. It is usually necessary to book such space.

Shared (hot) office

This operates on the same basis as a hot desk but in addition supports the need for occasional privacy, confidentiality or concentration. It is usually necessary to book hot offices.

Touchdown

Touchdowns are workbenches or other surfaces intended to support short-stay, 'drop-in' working; often (but not always) designed for use by employees standing up, they reflect the transitory nature of the work carried out at them. They are useful for visitors, and so are often placed near entrances or circulation routes.

Touchdown

Study booth/carrel

These are semi-open or enclosed shared (hot) desks located in quieter areas to support concentrated work.

Study booths

Formal meeting room

This is an enclosed room on the lines of the 'traditional' meeting room, with formal table and chairs. The room is, typically, well equipped in terms of technology support, with facilities for conference calls, presentations and video conferencing etc. Furniture might also be adaptable, ie tables can be re-configured to allow different styles of meeting to be held.

Informal meeting area

By this I mean an open, semi-open or even enclosed meeting space with a more informal feel, often with softer, upholstered furniture, and situated near main circulation routes and coffee-vending points – see the graphic below.

Informal meeting area

Quiet space

As the name suggests, this is a dedicated, enclosed or open area designed to provide a contrast with the interactive nature of the office. The aim is to support reflection and concentration, as shown below.

Quiet space

Project/breakout space

Open or enclosed, the project or breakout space is designed for and dedicated specifically to project and teamworking activities. It is usually set up to support interaction as well as individual work; furniture and fittings may be mobile and flexible to accommodate this. Whiteboards and pinboards also feature, to assist the development of ideas and sharing of knowledge. Such space may be allocated to a team or project to 'own' for a particular period.

Project/breakout space

Service area
This is a dedicated area for photocopying, printing and post etc, normally located centrally and part-enclosed to reduce noise to other areas.

Neighbourhood space
This term refers to the use of key circulation routes to provide a focus for interaction, with associated supporting facilities such as seating and coffee-vending points etc. In larger buildings, an atrium naturally provides such an opportunity, often through a 'street' feature with shops and cafés along its route, as illustrated opposite.

Some of the worksettings that we have described will be familiar; others may appear radically unfamiliar – but perhaps not so much as you may at first think. Often they do not even require new furniture or fittings. You may in fact have some already; others can be adapted quite simply from existing settings. In other words, it doesn't have to be a big deal in terms of cost or disruption to provide these facilities.

But what these concepts do require is a change in how people use and think about their workplace; and the way they are planned and put together is also a very important consideration.

Neighbourhood space

New layouts

The new worksettings should reflect both the *time* involved in certain tasks and the *nature* of those tasks, and so should be arranged accordingly. For example, touchdown areas designed for short-stay, 'drop-in' work may be positioned near the entrance to the workplace, whereas offices and study booths designed for longer-stay, more concentrated work may be positioned much deeper into the workplace away from the main circulation and noisier areas such as informal meeting spaces, open-plan workspaces and service areas.

Workspace that is used by people for long periods of time, such as 'owned' desks, should be positioned in the best part of the office in terms of space, light, air and noise. Such benefits are less essential in areas where people are working for just an hour or so.

All of this is simple common sense. It takes just a moment's reflection, for instance, to realise that, at home, the facilities in the kitchen and the way they are positioned are far more important than those in the spare room.

These changes can reverse some of the current status arrangements: for example, secretaries may end up getting the best-quality space, executives and managers sharing what is left. Some organisations may find this quite a challenge to their traditional working arrangements. For example, in the Civil Service and in many large corporations workspace has typically been allocated very precisely according to status –

INSTITUTE OF PERSONNEL
AND DEVELOPMENT

Customer Satisfaction Survey

*We would be grateful if you could spend a few minutes answering these questions and return the postcard to IPD. <u>Please use a black pen to answer.</u> **If you would like to receive a free IPD pen, please include your name and address.***

....

1. Title of book ....

2. Date of purchase: month .... year ....

3. How did you buy this book?
   ☐ Bookshop ☐ Mail order ☐ Exhibition

4. If ordered by mail, how long did it take to arrive:
   ☐ 1 week ☐ 2 weeks ☐ more than 2 weeks

5. Name of shop .... Town.. Country ....

6. Please grade the following according to their influence on your purchasing decision with 1 as least influential: (please tick)

	1	2	3	4	5
Title					
Publisher					
Author					
Price					
Subject					

7. On a scale of 1 to 5 (with 1 as poor & 5 as excellent) please give your impressions of the book in terms of: (please tick)

	1	2	3	4	5
Cover design					
Page design					
Paper/print quality					
Good value for money					

8. Did you find the book:
   Covers the subject in sufficient depth ☐ Yes ☐ No
   Useful for your work ☐ Yes ☐ No

9. Are you using this book to help:
   ☐ In your work ☐ Personal study ☐ Both ☐ Other (please state) ....

Please complete if you are using this as part of a course

10. Name of academic institution..

11. Name of course you are following? ....

12. Did you find this book relevant to the syllabus? ☐ Yes ☐ No ☐ Don't know

Thank you!

To receive regular information about IPD books and resources call 0181 263 3387.
Any data or information provided to the IPD for the purposes of membership and other Institute activities will be processed by means of a computer database or otherwise. You may, from time to time, receive business information relevant to your work from the Institute and its other activities. If you do not wish to receive such information please write to the IPD, giving your full name, address and postcode. The Institute does not make its membership lists available to any outside organisation.

2

Publishing Department

Institute of Personnel and Development

IPD House

Camp Road

Wimbledon

London

SW19 4BR

12 square metres for directors, nine square metres for managers, and six square metres for executives and administrative staff. In contrast to such traditional allocation of office space, the graphics below and on page 26 show how a combination of new-style worksettings may look.

Example layouts of new workplace settings

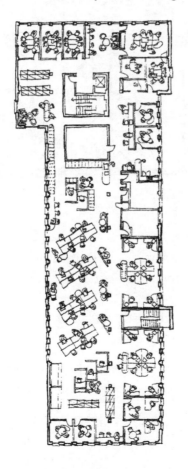

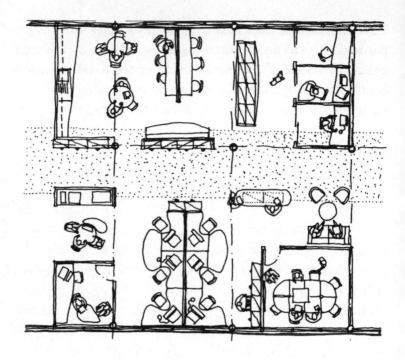

New protocols

Many of the worksettings described here are shared. This requires new protocols. In particular, it requires:

● adjusting workspace to meet individual needs, as appropriate

■ leaving workspace as found for others to use afterwards, including the clearing away of personal items and papers

▲ booking use of the workspace, where appropriate.

This requires in turn new ways of managing workspace, particularly in terms of booking systems and filing and storage policies – and also the introduction of clear-desk policies. Staff need preparation and guidance to cope with the transition to these concepts. I shall return to these important topics later.

In terms of sharing and booking space, it is important to recognise that office work can be both planned and spontaneous. Therefore it will be important to have some shared workspace that can be secured in advance, as well as having other shared workspace to be used on a non-bookable (first come, first served) basis. Getting this balance right is important, but it is something that can be easily adjusted through experience. Also, as a guide, up to 50 per cent of new workspace may be given over to shared, interactive non-desk space (such as informal/formal meeting areas). This is in sharp contrast with the way most offices currently operate.

Increasingly, these new ways of managing workspace are supported and co-ordinated by an almost hotel-style of operation – complete with a concierge, as a new style of office manager.

Buzzwords and jargon

I am conscious of having already started to introduce some new workplace jargon – like touchdowns, carrels and concierge – which you may not be familiar with. Collectively, these new workplace concepts, along with the associated new working practices (such as wise-working and nomadic working), have given rise to a whole new lexicon of trendy buzzwords.

These words are great for impressing (or confusing) your friends and colleagues. But most of these new terms are really just variations on the same theme: new ways of describing work without the constraints of traditional understandings of time and place. This world is very far removed from the hide-bound ideas and monotony of the 'clerical factory'.

Although to the uninitiated these terms imply an element of gimmickry and fad, we should not forget that the concepts and principles behind them are serious and here to stay – so ignore them at your peril!

feng shui and fishtanks   3

Making a difference through detail and design

Design is one of the most powerful change tools that you
have. Of course, an office should be well planned and
functional but, in addition to that, the right design can have
a positive influence on moods and attitudes.

The power of design

Traditionally, a 'safe' approach is taken in the workplace to
décor, colour, fittings and fixtures. In a way this is strange,
because we all like colour, texture, softness, warmth, light,
creativity and variety. Take our homes, or the restaurants
and hotels we choose: design, style and appearance always
matter – and it doesn't always have to be expensive to achieve
a harmonious balance of these elements. So why can't we
apply the same principles to the workplace?

Senses at work

Quite logically, the main focus of workplace design is on *visual*
attractiveness (as well as pure functionality). Basic layout
considerations have been covered in Chapter 2; but one other
aspect yet to be considered is the avoidance of straight lines
and very obvious, regular layouts. Positioning desks at angles,

having curved walls or partitioning and creating thoughtful circulation routes can significantly add to the visual interest of our surroundings. This is a trick that painters, photographers and landscape gardeners use to increase the visual appeal of their creations: by ensuring that there is more than one route through the scene they create, they give the eye choice and encourage it to linger and discover more.

However, there are other senses that may be exploited (with care) – for example:

● the sound of running water or soft music

■ the feel of soft furnishings or fresh air

▲ the smell of fresh flowers or coffee.

This all adds to the 'feel' of the workplace and helps achieve a more relaxing, comfortable and stimulating environment.

A number of open-plan offices, such as Glaxo Wellcome's offices at Stockley Park, have running water features with lush, almost tropical, foliage in atriums; the flow of water can be heard, seen and sensed throughout the whole building. The effect is calming and natural. But avoid plastic plants and pots – or even real plants that look plastic!

I have also seen offices that provide a sheltered, protected area that gives a feel of the outside world although still within the office complex; such an area can be used for informal meetings or reflection with the benefits of real fresh air and sunlight. The new Government Buildings at The Hague have a roof that can be moved back when the weather permits – so that the sky provides the office ceiling! (If I recall correctly, some netting was necessary to keep birds from enjoying the office environment too.)

Style and quality
The overall style and quality of furniture and fittings are very important. Assuming that what you develop is something that is going to be well used and needs to last, then durability and ease of maintenance are important considerations. It is worth investing properly.

Don't be afraid: quality does not always have to mean high expense. Often it is just about making sensible choices. Beware of getting too carried away with the latest trends, particularly when it comes to substantial items such as furniture. Funky but fragile chairs and sexy but odd-shaped desks may look good, but they may also not last. Even if they do, they may not look quite so trendy after a while – so remember, fashions change!

You can also make good use of what you already have and build on that. This applies to furnishings, flooring, colour schemes etc – provided, of course, that what you have is not too ghastly!

Colour

You can use painted walls, features and accessories to make your visual statement. They are easily updated, and it is relatively inexpensive to do so. You can sensibly balance to good effect contemporary colours and features with more enduring items of furniture.

Strong colours can of course be very powerful – blue, red, green, yellow, orange – but there are certain rules about combinations that it would be wise to observe ('Blue and green should not be seen...'). There are complementary families of colours, which most suppliers provide basic guidance about.

Although input from professional interior designers can be useful, you can do a lot yourself just by using common sense. However, do avoid using attractive décor as no more than a superficial cover-up. No matter how attractive, it will not compensate for bad overall layout and planning of your workspace.

Colour can also be used to define different areas of the workplace, and even to encourage different moods. One office that I remember had blue for thinking and reflection, red for action and communication, green for learning and knowledge, and yellow for eating and relaxation. You may have other personal associations with colours.

Of course, colours are not just confined to walls. Floors can also feature strong colour to break up and distinguish different spaces or zones within the workplace. Very often you can retain the majority of existing floor coverings but introduce a new type of finish to great effect in one or two key areas only – for example, by using vinyl in the café or main circulation routes.

Ceilings can also be partly replaced with different features to add visual interest and variety – perhaps with lower or different-shaped features over significant areas of the workplace, such as the entrance or main circulation route. Avoid strong colours on ceilings, though.

Take care not to overdo strong colours on walls either. Splashes of colour can often be more attractive. British Airways' Waterside offices near Heathrow provide an effective example: predominately white walls are broken up with just the odd wall or pillar picked out in a strong, themed colour.

British Airways' Waterside is also a good example of where such natural materials as wood, stone, plants and trees – and of course water – have been used to great impact in their so-called 'street'. With its extensive glass roof, you feel 'outside' even though in the middle of the building – just as if you were walking in a real outdoor street. Even the weather and light can influence the mood of this key part of BA's working environment.

Air, light and temperature

Other aspects of comfort levels in the office are affected by air, light and temperature – artificial and natural. It is always preferable for staff to be able to control the features of their immediate working environment. Make the most of daylight, but bear in mind the effect of strong sunshine. Also, a view is very important psychologically to staff – so don't block things out! Supplementary lighting, including desk task lighting, can be used to add mood, interest and choice for staff.

Take account of existing heating and air conditioning arrangements if you intend to knock down or add walls. You may upset the intended flow of air or heat, and so adjustments may be needed.

The effectiveness of a well-designed, attractive office can be completely undermined if staff become uncomfortable because of temperature extremes, drafts, stuffiness and so on. Setting these things right can be costly; and because they cannot be seen, there is a temptation to overlook them in the quest for more immediately appreciated visual improvements. But this is a fundamental aspect to get right.

Features and finishing touches

The importance of features and finishing touches is often neglected. They generally cost very little but can also send out a strong message about style and image, and even care for employees.

Once again, think about what we do in our everyday lives. We add finishing touches to our homes, such as artworks, ornaments, flowers and so on, in order to add character, style and interest – to make them *ours*. The same principle applies in the workplace – and if staff can have some involvement in the choices, then the impact, pride and sense of 'ownership' can be even greater. We are talking about details as simple as flowers, projected images, clocks, cushions, artwork and even the provision of decent coffee or other beverages.

Artwork is always a good option, and there is a wide range of ways of sourcing artwork – with options to change and refresh them on a regular basis. BBC Broadcast in London, for example, displayed large colourful pieces by local artists in their new workspace in Broadcasting House – with many for sale. Such was their popularity, many pieces were sold to staff within a few months.

Another effective feature is for organisations to display items linked to its business or outputs – a powerful reminder to staff of the business purpose and achievements and a way of adding to corporate pride. Features such as these are often to be found in reception areas, but there is no reason why displays should not be sited elsewhere – in staff restaurants, meeting spaces and internal corridors – to give a feel of corporate history and staff pride. BBC Broadcast again provides a good example here – where old copies of the *Radio Times* and radio sets are displayed alongside plasma screens showing the very latest digital outputs.

What does your workplace tell you, your colleagues or your visitors about your business activities and achievements?

Little things count

In all the projects I have worked on, I have found that it is often the little things that make the biggest impact on staff: I have had more positive feedback and e-mail about cushions and coffee-machines than anything else! The point is that the cost of these items is tiny compared with the significant sums spent on furniture or technology, which (ironically) seemed almost to be taken for granted.

This is not to undermine the value of those greater expenses. They are usually essential. But the surprise element of those finishing touches can be powerful – and all the more effective if they reflect staff involvement and ideas.

So, when planning and spending your budget, do leave a little bit for those shopping trips to Habitat and Ikea, the art gallery and the aquarium! And don't forget little details like new desk filing trays and wastepaper bins – you won't want the ugly old ones staying around to spoil the effect!

Dressing for your workplace

An interesting dimension to style is the way we look. To what extent does our appearance affect the feel, image and performance of the workplace? To what extent does formal, informal or uniform dress harmonise with a given workplace?

I do not have all the answers here – and, anyway, the whole question is well beyond the scope of this book. What I can say, however, is that increasingly I can see a very positive freedom of choice emerging in many workplaces, where formally and informally dressed staff work comfortably together – the code being determined purely by 'what they are doing' and 'whom they are seeing' that day.

This 'match-the-task' approach to clothing seems to me complementary to the flexibility and choice of the new workplace: it helps put people at ease, removes status-driven hierarchy and reflects the range of activities being performed.

Many companies have introduced the concept of 'dressing down' on certain days of the week only, usually a Friday. Some have introduced 'down-dressing' as a permanent matter of policy across the organisation. Interestingly, this can give rise to problems for some employees, because clothing (executive suits and ties) have been used as a status symbol as much as the enclosed 'single occupancy' office has.

Feng shui

As the title to this chapter suggests, it would be wrong to write about making a difference to the workplace through layout and design without making reference to *feng shui*. It has attracted increasing interest in recent years, and its practices are being enthusiastically applied.

For the uninitiated, *feng shui* is a method of arranging an environment to the benefit of its users. Benefits are supposed to come in the form of health, happiness and wealth. Based on ancient Chinese philosophy, *feng shui* has, it seems to me, some rather complicated connections with directions, elements, animals, numbers and the calendar. It is an art that requires knowledge and skills.

The principles behind it lie in the appropriate channelling and manipulation of energy known as *ch'i*. It recognises both negative and positive energy (called *yin* and *yang* respectively) and the importance of getting the right balance of such energy.

In the simplest of terms, the 'flow' and balance of energy or *ch'i* is influenced by the positioning and form of physical matter. So both the way you lay out space and the materials you use are very important.

Good and bad *ch'i*

Factors that influence a 'good' and 'bad' flow of *ch'i* include the following:

Good	Bad
● brightness	● darkness
▣ order	▣ confusion
▲ calm	▲ clutter
◉ curves	◉ straight lines
● cleanliness	● harsh noise
● freedom (no direction imposed)	● disorder
▣ welcome/guidance	▣ being squeezed
▲ usefulness	▲ neglect
◉ living things (plants, pets)	◉ corners
● movement	● stagnation

Here are some other interesting points relevant to the office:

● Colour may be used thematically (for example, red to encourage energy, light blue for calm)

▣ People should not sit with their backs to the door.

▲ People should not face blank walls.

◉ Mirrors should be used to reflect light and good views.

● Fish, round-leafed plants and the colour red all have positive links to money.

Intuition

I am not an expert on *feng shui*, but I am a great believer in common sense. My empathy with much of what I have read about this philosophy is based upon just that. And it has certainly provided me with some valuable reassurance about my own intuition.

Although I am confident that the guidelines in this book will help you to improve the efficiency and effectiveness of your working environment, I cannot guarantee the true health, wealth and happiness that *feng shui* promises. So there may well be true added value in pursuing this area further!

Fishtanks

This brings me, improbably, to fishtanks – highly approved within *feng shui* for bringing life and movement into the environment. There is an effective virtual-reality fishtank in the reception of NEC in Livingston, Scotland, and one of Glaxo Wellcome's offices near Heathrow has an amazing fishpond as a focal point in the middle of its workplace – complete with giant fish and tropical fauna.

On one of my projects, the staff suggested a fishtank be placed in their café. The results were extraordinary. Yes, the fish provided an attractive and soothing feature; but they also evoked a real sense of ownership and care in the office, embodied by the self-appointed 'fish team' set up to look after the piscine arrivals. Although not directly business-related, this was the first of a number of interdepartmental teams that we were to see emerge in the new workplace. The fish provided a focal point and brought people together.

However, we quickly learnt that we were not fish experts, because some of the fish started to die – probably through too much attention, love and food! So we found someone in the organisation to do the job who really was an expert. Another lesson learnt.

Fun

I suppose that fun is the last point you might expect on this topic: workplaces can have a reputation for being stern, boring and serious places. But they can also be enjoyable too. After all, a break from the intensity of our busy working lives can be welcome and often increases our productivity. So add a bit of humour and fun – perhaps through artwork or temporary features and displays. The noticeboard is always a good place to start. At the very least, a couple of Dilbert™ cartoons remind people about the old office world of cubicles, hierarchy and bureaucracy that (hopefully) they have now escaped from!

A great example of what I am talking about may be found at the headquarters of the Twynstra Group (the parent company of DEGW) at Amersfoort in the Netherlands. On display is artwork that moves and reacts to passers-by – which is always guaranteed to raise a smile with visitors and staff alike!

getting it right

4

Finding the right solutions for you, your organisation and your budget

I have said quite a bit so far about the context of workplace change and emerging new workplace concepts and design ideas. It all points toward a drive for improvement in terms of quality, efficiency and effectiveness – and business improvement should be at the heart of any organisational or workplace change. But remember, *change* and *improvement* are not necessarily the same thing.

You need to think very carefully about what workplace changes you make – and how you make them. They should be based on sound business reasoning. They must be well planned and sustainable. So what, for you, will be the right solution?

The right solution

The wide range of workplace options to consider when transforming your workplace requires some important decisions. This is exciting but also, perhaps, a little daunting. The thing to bear in mind is that there are no fixed rules – you are better off going instead for a 'pick and mix' approach that gives you maximum flexibility in what you do. But you still need to make the right choices *for you*. Finding the right solution or model to match the business needs of your organisation and its culture is the most important decision you make, second only to the way you decide then to implement that change. In other words, it is important first to assess the situation and then to consult.

Let's look more closely now at these considerations.

Assessing the requirements

It would be foolish to implement any workplace change without having properly taken into account the people who use that space and the work that they do in it. But simply asking people what they want or need is not always appropriate. Ask anybody what they want and they will nearly always request a newer and bigger version of what they have already got. Their requirements are likely to be based only upon their current experiences. Equally, what they ask for may be neither practical nor affordable – and by asking the wrong questions you may raise unrealistic expectations that, by definition, cannot be met.

Consultation

It is essential that you consult staff. But think carefully about how you do this. Ask about work processes, working practices, interaction, technology needs and business aspirations; don't just ask about personal preferences or the size, shape and preferred colour of desks!

Try also to understand how the current workspace is used and how well it performs. The workspace utilisation studies (see page 7) are a valuable part of this picture. To find out how well workspaces fulfil their intended roles and how staff feel about them, you can carry out interviews, workshops and questionnaires and, of course, make your own observations.

You must also continue to consult and offer input and choices as your project develops. This way it becomes possible to manage expectations and maintain staff involvement, which are the key to success.

Workstyles

Everyone employed in an office has a workstyle that reflects the way they use their workspace and the technology associated with it. Your consultation process and the utilisation study should reveal the sort of workstyles current in your team or organisation. There are likely to be just three main ones:

- staff extensively office- and desk-based, often dealing with process work – for example, administrative staff

- staff primarily office-based but often at meetings or away from their desks for periods of time, ie highly interactive workers who also need to concentrate – for example, executive staff

▲ staff frequently away from their offices or desks, perhaps working at other locations or in meetings but still needing to use offices or desks at some time and also needing confidentiality and concentration – for example, managers.

Your ideal workplace solution has to reflect and support all these workstyles. Whether it does or not is the real test of the model you select.

Personalities

Within these workstyles you will also get a range of personalities that typify particular ways of working. In some cases, these personalities will be helpful; in others, they may provide a challenge. Whichever it is, you need to be aware of and watch out for them, so that you can focus your efforts accordingly.

Here are some that I am sure you will recognise:

● the *paper-hoarder* – the one who likes to keep copies of everything for everybody, usually in a very organised way – and whose requirements for cabinet, drawer and shelf space would be enough the fill a normal office in its own right. This person will find a clear-desk policy a challenge – but may have some good ideas on new systems for filing, archiving and retrieval.

■ the *nester* – the one who also likes paper, as well as lots of other items, including furry toy animals and posters –

and likes to be surrounded by all these personal effects, usually in a very disorganised and cluttered manner. This person may feel insecure in the new workspace at first and so will need to find new ways of feeling comfortable.

▲ the *territorial terrier* – the one for whom ownership of defendable personal space is the priority; if this person doesn't have his or her own office, 'walls' will be created out of filing cabinets, screens and plants to mark out territory. This person hates open-plan offices and lots of glass but can be brought to accept the concept of sharing open space if it is made clear that the whole office is as much his or hers to use as anybody else's.

● the *status king* – the one to whom size really does matter, in terms of office space, desk, the number of windows in the room etc. This person will need help to recognise that new symbols, such as flexibility and freedom, can replace the existing hierarchical ones.

● the *control freak* – the one who needs instant access to everything, including staff – who should ideally always be in view and available. Flexible working is OK – as long as nobody else does it! New ways of managing staff and productivity need to be learnt here.

● the *worrier* – the one whose sense of a lack of information, context, and understanding can lead to concerns that are often blown out of proportion. This person is prone to rumour-spreading and mere gossip. But the right communication and involvement should ensure that this personality can work for, not against, you.

■ the *influencer* – the one who, though not necessarily senior, seems to have the ear and respect of everyone and who is a leader others will follow. An ideal person to get on-side and use as a role model.

▲ the *virtual reality nomad* – the one who exercises an extreme example of flexible working, being rarely seen, carrying no papers and requiring no desk or filing space. You may think that such a person is almost too good to be true, so watch out for the catch, but he or she can be an inspiration to others.

Sponsorship

One of the most common reasons for the failure of workplace-change projects is a lack of senior-level commitment. The latter is essential to make things happen in the first place and, more importantly, to sustain the changes in the longer term.

This is a matter of involving your manager, director or, depending on the scale of the project, your chief executive. Don't be daunted: you may get more enthusiasm and ownership than you expect from this level. These people are going to spot a business winner when they see it, and your proposal may just be the initiative they are looking for.

The lesson is clear: get the right senior people involved in the changes as far as you can. This will have a powerful knock-on effect with others lower down the pecking-order, particularly where there is resistance.

You probably know where resistance is likely to come from in your team or organisation – to be blunt, you know who the dinosaurs are. A peer or senior colleague will probably have more influence on such people than you, so use this fact to your advantage. Find senior role models – people willing to put the changes into practice – to help you.

Teamwork

Depending on the size and scope of your project and depending on your role, you may need to enlist the help of others to help you transform your workplace. On larger projects the typical internal disciplines that need to contribute are:

- facilities management
- personnel/HR
- information technology (IT)
- communications
- change (if this discipline formally exists where you are).

As well as the valuable knowledge these people can bring to your project, you will make better progress with them on your side. From my experience, if they are not involved such experts can often be suspicious of what you are doing, which will obviously work against you. It is working together that gets results.

Use of specialists

In addition to what has been suggested so far, external expertise will probably be required in planning, designing and implementing change. The trick is however to balance internal and external resources and specialists to get the best value and results for your project.

Here is a summary of likely distinctions to assist in your considerations here but, remember, the situation differs for every organisation:

Internal
- health and safety
- information and communication technology (ICT)
- storage and filing arrangements
- business case
- (management of) training and change management

External
- space-usage studies
- space selection and assessment
- space-planning
- furniture procurement
- design
- structural, electrical or mechanical work
- support of training/ change management

Certain activities are definitely better handled internally. For example, staff communication and involvement are far more effective if they are seen to be internally driven, even if you get external advice to help you. Remember, staff do not usually appreciate having external consultants 'doing it to them'. (I cover more about communication and staff involvement in the next chapter.)

Efficiency v effectiveness

The temptation is often to focus on *efficiency* when looking to transform your workplace. This is partly owing to the inevitable pressures to justify the cost (or savings) involved in what you want to do, but it is a mistake to lay the emphasis here.

There is usually no doubt that efficiencies can be made – notably through the sharing of workspace, where appropriate. Such efficiencies and their attendant savings can be effected with reasonable ease, but they should not be the focus of your approach. If they are, it may arouse suspicion among staff about the motives for change.

A successful change programme provides immediate benefits. But too much emphasis on efficiency above all else will not bring long-term, sustainable benefits. The more substantial benefits are instead those based on *effectiveness*. The problem is that such benefits are harder to quantify and take longer to realise. They are typically expressed by 'soft' measures based on perceptions and feelings. Creativity, motivation, staff retention and staff attraction are all examples of such benefits. They are less tangible than the benefits of efficiency, but they are crucial.

So get the right balance between efficiency and effectiveness. Don't fall into the trap of having to justify everything only in terms of cost efficiencies. You shouldn't need to. (I say a little more about measures of success in Chapter 6.)

Keeping your costs down

Workplace change projects are no exception to many other projects: they can eat money up and unexpected costs always emerge, so they need to be financially well managed and monitored. Contingency should also be built in. (There is more on costing your implementation in the next chapter.)

There are, of course, ways of keeping costs down – by, for instance, using existing furniture, fittings and technology, using internal resources, being creative and using common sense. Communicating with and supporting your people may be one of the most valuable investments you make – and much of this is just about providing proper time and planning. Also, don't overlook all those little details that can make such a big difference but cost very little.

But be careful not to underfund your initiative. You can do more damage than good by starving it of the necessary resources. Better not even to start if you have to compromise your objectives and plans too much.

Passion

One of the most important things you need to do is to develop your vision and the principles underlying it clearly. But clarity alone is not enough: you must be determined about what you want to do and to achieve. Believe in what you are doing – and be passionate about it! Make your commitment evident during your communications with others; if you do so, your feelings will be infectious.

Remember, vision alone changes nothing. But vision with passion can change the world.

making it happen 5

Practical steps to successful implementation

By now you should have a good idea of the sort of changes you want to make – and, most importantly, the reasons. But how do you best implement your vision?

The answer lies in the two themes of this chapter – the *physical transformation* and the *people transformation*. I cannot emphasise enough the importance of tackling both these interlinked aspects, no matter how big or small your project is.

The physical transformation

Planning

You should plan the physical implementation of your project very carefully – particularly for larger projects. You have to understand the full scope of the work involved and set realistic time-scales within which it is all to happen.

Time-scales should recognise delays often inherent in the time of year (Christmas holidays, for example) as well as lead-in time for ordering furniture. Despite the fact that this is all simple, common sense, it is often overlooked in the enthusiasm to move forward.

You also need to identify, plan and secure the resources you need to deliver the project properly – both financial and human resources.

Link your plan to your vision and objectives, and communicate it appropriately – with passion – remembering the key role that people have in what you are trying to achieve.

Size matters

Changes can be made both to your own workstation or office and by demonstrating to others better ways of doing things. However, changes across a whole team or department are much more effective and valuable. It is hard to start a revolution on your own!

This question of scale reflects the fact that only at a certain level do the important office dynamics and diversity really come into play. But you should also be careful about trying to do too much at once.

Where a whole office or organisation is to be transformed, the idea of introducing the changes in 'bite-size' chunks or through an initial pilot approach can be extremely useful.

Piloting

A pilot also means you can try out the concepts in a reasonably safe and secure environment – and allows the organisation to take the time to learn and to adapt through experience. An ideal size of pilot to give a useful range of feedback might be one involving anything from 20 to 100 staff.

The value of pilots should not just be limited to those directly affected. For instance, you can:

● get the whole organisation involved

▣ hold open days

▲ place facilities within the pilot that others will need to access – like specialist equipment or resources.

But, in all this, you must allow others to become familiar with the new concepts; avoid creating an 'us and them' situation in pushing through the changes.

It is a good idea to set up a pilot workspace somewhere easily accessible and highly visible if you want to achieve wider impact and involvement. At Scottish Enterprise I took over a disused shop area on the ground floor of the head office to create the 'Workplace of the Future' project. The space was a physical challenge, but it was readily available and highly visible.

It is also important to ensure that it is a true pilot – in other words, that you build in ways of evaluating what has been done and how it is working.

Finding people

Choosing the staff to become involved in a pilot is, to state the obvious, an important consideration. It is best to get a cross-section of staff involved so that a range of disciplines and views is represented. Of course, have some who you are confident will make it work, but also have some of those whom you expect to struggle. The messages from the pilot will be all the stronger and more valuable because of that mix. But don't break up teams to secure involvement, because this will place unnecessary and unrealistic strains on working practices.

Planning the workspace

You also need to find the right space to transform. If this is your existing workspace, there will be some challenges. You may wish to consider some form of alternative or 'decanting' space while any major physical works are undertaken.

Don't forget to take photos of the existing space before you embark on the changes – these can be a valuable reminder of where you have come from.

Remember, furthermore, to calculate the space you need with care. Don't make comparisons with existing space allocations: that is likely to reflect the old working world you are trying to leave behind.

If you are introducing a degree of sharing, then logically you should need less space. However, you may also be introducing additional concepts. The net effect may still be less space, but it needs to be thought through very carefully.

In planning the space, consider the following:

● the characteristics of the available space – its size, position, condition, services and access

■ the number of staff involved, their workstyles and their aspirations for the future – this might also include likely visitors

▲ the range of worksettings required, linked to the above – recognising the diversity and dynamics involved

● the overall image and style required.

You should also build in adaptability, which may affect your decisions about services (power, data and voice), furniture and fittings.

Remember, extremes either of open-plan or cellular space are unlikely to be appropriate, whereas a balance of open and enclosed space may well be – so don't rush to knock down all those walls!

An open environment is essential to support the desired levels of interaction, but enclosed space is also precious in terms of allowing complementary, quiet concentration or confidential work. Ideally that sort of space should be available to all, not just senior staff; therefore many elements of existing offices remain valid – it is just a matter of how that space is owned and used that may need to change.

However, enclosed space should ideally not compromise the quality of open space. For example, traditional lay-outs often rob daylight from open space by putting offices on the outside walls. Maximise the amount of natural daylight, so that if you have any of those status-driven corner offices, they *will* need to go.

Proper space-planning of desks and all worksettings is required. This is best done by the appropriate specialists. Good planning can help you make the most of the available space and also ensure that worksettings are positioned correctly to maximise effectiveness, recognising both the occupancy time and the type of tasks involved.

The worksettings

The exact configuration of worksettings in your new workspace depends very much on the workstyles of the staff and the degree of sharing that is felt appropriate. Your workspace utilisation studies (see Chapter 1) should assist you here. But the likelihood is that a suitable balance of all worksettings will be required.

Where desk-sharing is appropriate, a reasonable initial approach to take is to plan a sharing ratio of 1:3. As long as other shared worksettings, such as touchdowns and study booths, are in place, there should always be enough room for staff to work in, even if everyone turns up.

When trying to assess the budget for your implementation, a useful basic approach is to calculate the cost of providing each worksetting and then multiply accordingly. These costs ought to include furniture, fittings, linked technology etc. More general infrastructural costs then need to be added, as required – such as services, cabling, lighting, decoration and mechanical and engineering aspects like heating and ventilation. A lot depends on whether you are transforming existing office space that is in reasonable condition or creating a new office from scratch.

Other models
You may find it useful to look at what other companies have implemented. There are lots of good examples around – some of them are listed at the end of this book (see the Appendix). But simply copying what has been done elsewhere is not recommended. You must find your own model – one that reflects the needs and culture of *your* organisation.

Furniture and fittings
Furniture is an important element of any office workplace environment, but the dominance of the desk as the only worksetting is now being seriously challenged.

New worksettings could include touchdown areas to support short-term, nomadic working; break-out areas in open plan to encourage informal and spontaneous interaction; and flexible enclosed spaces to allow more focused meetings or for team, individual and project working. These areas can be fitted out relatively cheaply – perhaps with specially made joinery items (for example, touchdown areas made out of cheap but versatile medium density fibreboard, or MDF).

Although a softer, more domestic style is appropriate to some of these new worksettings, don't forget the heavy wear that office furniture has to endure. Buy suitably robust items.

Health and safety

Many offices that I see have fairly old furniture, particularly the desks – some well overdue for replacement, if only because of their lack of compliance with health and safety regulations. So use the opportunity to check whether you are meeting EU standards and regulations, and replace items where you can. It is now illegal, for example, not to contain cables properly, to have the wrong height of desk, or not to provide ample legroom for manoeuvre between pedestals.

Health and safety is an essential aspect in the establishment and running of any office – and professional advice is required here. Most organisations have a nominated internal specialist, but if yours does not, engage external help. There are strict regulations covering the safety and comfort of staff in the office.

Much of this still, unfortunately, relates to the older 'clerical factory' style of office – where it is assumed that staff are fixed to their desks and PCs all day. So recognise the implications of increased mobility and shorter-stay working when interpreting the regulations and guidelines.

It is essential that you do not forget the needs of staff with disabilities, especially now that such matters are covered by legislation. Appropriate access for the disabled and the provision of adjustable desking and seating are now a requirement, not an option.

Desks and hot-desking

First off, don't assume that hot-desking is only for staff who spend significant time away from the office. Office-based staff too can benefit from the dynamism of such schemes, which allow them to move around the office and support the building of networks and multi-project working. Always keep your options open. But what sort of desks should you get?

Existing desks can, of course, still be used. However, depending on their age and style (and aside from health and safety considerations), it may be difficult or just impossible to re-configure them so that they support such new concepts as desk-sharing (hot-desking).

New desks, though, can make a big difference to planning, appearance and functionality. But make sure that you adopt a standard, consistent, single-status approach here, so that staff can move around static furniture and so that you avoid the need for all those 'churn'-related furniture-moving antics. Remember, too, that office needs evolve: it is vital that you use a system that allows for add-ons, so that desks can easily be customised (for example, to provide more meeting space).

If you are going for new desks, avoid buying ones with pedestals or drawers attached. This immediately links a person to that desk through the storage of personal papers and items – clearly not a good idea if you are operating hot-desking arrangements. Even where staff have their own desks, *non*-attached pedestals enable those desks to become hot desks in the future. Things can change in this area very quickly!

But do be wary: experience has shown me that pedestals (even if they are described as 'mobile') are not designed for frequent movement and are awkward to move if full. They often get abandoned all over the place, causing a hazard, and can require special 'parking space' when not in use or left overnight. This takes up very valuable floorspace. I would strongly suggest that nearby stackable storage drawers be provided for the personal papers and effects of staff. 'Carrying boxes' or similar devices can be provided to assist staff in carrying items around the office. This solution is often more practical than having mobile pedestals or storage trolleys moved around the office.

You should consider providing basic stationery items at desks or at local zones to support shared desking. Often the absence of such small items as staplers, pens and hole-punchers is the cause of much frustration, and make mobile staff long for the reliability of an 'owned' desk.

A final word: avoid buying desks that are 'over-designed' – ones that are too trendy or actually designed for domestic use. They are likely to be less robust and may quickly look dated. Desks are an investment that should last and ideally be functional – even timeless – in their design.

What sort of desks and furniture do you have at present?

Is the furniture re-usable?

Does it comply with EU health and safety standards, particularly in terms of cable management?

Will it support or hinder the transformations you want to make?

Chairs

Where staff are expected to work in the one place for substantial periods of time, suitable task chairs are required. Softer, more informal seating might be provided in short-stay areas.

There are a number of very good furniture suppliers out there, so do shop around for the best options and deals – and remember to use the buying power that your organisation as a whole commands.

Information and communication technology (ICT)

Technology is an essential tool for any organisation and a key enabler for much of the flexibility demanded by the modern office. Laptop and palmtop computers, flat-screens, cableless equipment, intranets, mobile telephones, voice-mail and voice-recognition are becoming more and more affordable. So, if you are not already familiar with these facilities, start to familiarise yourself now!

However, you do not necessarily need to have leading-edge technology to run an effective, modern office. Indeed, much of the existing technology within organisations is underused. Hot-desking can still operate successfully with desktop PCs and traditional telephones. As with the physical elements of the office environment, it is *how* you use these resources that is important.

It is beyond the scope of this book to go into IT in detail, but if I had to pick out some key developments to add value, I would suggest the following:

- *flat screens* – increasingly more affordable, providing a good-quality display and freeing up valuable desk space

- *cableless desk accessories* – mouse, keyboard, links to printers and even networks – again these simplify and increase the flexibility of desk usage

- *laptop* PCs – enabling greater mobility for staff, both outside and (let's not forget) *inside* the office – but do note that health and safety considerations require links to an adjustable screen and keyboard for more *continuous* PC working

- *cordless telephones* – operating inside the office as well as (ideally) outside. This is one of the most valuable of new developments, in my view, because it truly releases staff from being tied to their desks and takes the strain from those left fielding calls for their nomadic colleagues.

Also, don't forget that all mobile equipment requires greater security – but there are some good padlock-type devices. Invest in them.

Storage and filing

One of the biggest practical challenges you will face will be storage and filing. Without doubt, most workplaces have far too much of both and it is often in the form of clutter – papers and files that have overspilled, in an unorganised way, onto desks, floors, shelves and any other free space to be found. Clearance of this alone has a dramatic impact. In fact if you did *only* this, you would probably still make a significant transformation to your workplace!

The symptoms of storage getting out of hand are simple and obvious:

- unnecessary duplication of documentation across teams due to lack of trust or co-ordination

- unnecessary duplication of paper and electronic storage

- inadequate archiving and/or retrieval systems

- inadequate or inappropriate personal and/or team storage and filing facilities

- lack of effective and reliable local stationery provision (leads to hoarding)

- lack of personal organisation and efficiency.

Most of these symptoms can be tackled easily, with nothing more than proper organisation and common sense. But if you really are planning to transform your workplace, take the opportunity to address these issues: you will find the proposed change the perfect catalyst to get staff to focus on them.

You can even make it fun. British Airways encouraged staff to clear out unnecessary paper before the move to their new Waterside office, monitored the levels of discarded paperwork and linked this to charity donations. I have also heard about one company that made a visual feature of its shredding and recycling process – blowing the shredded paper around the office through highly visible transparent tubes.

The best approach here is to provide a standard, but reduced, level of *personal* and *team* storage. Advise staff well in advance (as part of your communication programme) and support them in:

- recognising the distinctions between these two types of storage

- organising and rationalising their storage accordingly by helping to identify opportunities to share, store electronically, archive and, importantly, throw out.

Of course, you do not have to wait. Clearance should start well before any move into new workspace, and there is no reason for not adopting clear-desk policies also. The bonus is that a clear-out provides a great chance for staff to try out the new practices.

Clear-desk policy

A clear-desk policy is essential for any form of hot-desking and shared worksettings. But I think it can, and should, be applied to all desks and work areas, whatever the 'ownership' position. It improves personal efficiency, security, appearance and future flexibility. Even an 'owned desk' can be more comfortably used by others if the desk is kept clear.

Set up some precise guidelines on this protocol to ensure clarity and find a way of (gently) enforcing it by arranging for left items to be removed. These items can then either be thrown away or left for re-claiming, depending on how ruthless you want to be! A 'clear' policy should also be extended to floors, shelves and corridors – so that a displacement factor does not set in and undermine what you are trying to do.

So much for the physical aspects of transforming your workplace; now for the important *people* aspects.

The people transformation

People, being the most important ingredient in the workplace, are the key to your success – or the reason for your failure.

Workplace emotions

Many of the difficulties of trying to update an office environment can be blamed on ourselves – as both the users and designers of workspace. By trying to keep people happy we have tended to adopt a 'safe' approach to the workplace and deliberately avoided tackling some of the deep-held emotions linked to the use and 'ownership' of workspace.

You may have already come across the *'That's* my *desk and* my *office – how dare you change things!'* response. (Maybe this has even been your own reaction at one time or another.) Many staff spend the biggest proportion of their working lives in these spaces, so no wonder they can get a little touchy about them. Also, in these times of rapid business change, the office can often provide a reassuringly constant feature in people's working lives; hence change in this area is often resisted even more than alterations in structure, systems and processes.

The moral is clear: handle workplace change with care. The aim of a change programme is to capture that strong sense of ownership but apply it to change rather than maintenance of the status quo.

Keeping things positive

It is, as we have seen, very likely that you will encounter some negativity and resistance, but if you regard this as a natural reaction it is possible to adopt a positive approach.

Remember that people will, quite naturally, always be looking from the 'What's in it for me?' viewpoint: 'How will the changes affect me? Where shall I sit? How will this affect my job?' Don't ignore that aspect, but acknowledge and respond to it both in the way you communicate and in what you communicate. People are not necessarily implacably resistant to change – but they may well be to *being changed*. They need to be involved and consulted, and to have proper time to accept, adjust and prepare.

> Think about other changes that have taken place in your organisation and ask yourself these questions:
>
> How were these handled?
>
> Were they successful?
>
> What went well?
>
> What went badly?

Change management

Consultation, communication, involvement and support are the fundamental components of a workplace-related change management programme. As with any major change, applying structure and planning to these activities helps enormously in securing a smooth transition and ensuring that staff 'buy into' the changes early on.

Such a programme of winning hearts and minds should be undertaken in parallel with the change to the physical workplace – but remember to start these 'psychological' initiatives in good time. Too often they are left to the last minute and embarked upon only as a reaction to resistance.

This parallel approach can best be described in the following terms:

- preparing the *workplace* for the people – *the traditional, physical works programme*
- preparing the *people* for the workplace – *the related change-management programme.*

It is also important to recognise the typical stages in the change process. For example, there is no point in trying to secure staff ownership and commitment before you have taken them through a basic awareness of the context and the reasoning for the changes – and allowed time for these to be understood and accepted. A common fault is that people jump straight in, only to be disappointed by the reaction they get. The graphics opposite represent the processes involved.

The stages of the change management process

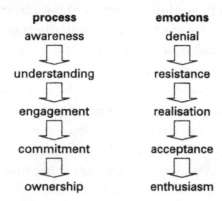

Overview of a typical workplace change management programme

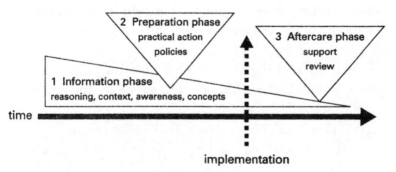

It is useful to think about the change process as a *journey, not a destination*. This reflects the reality of change – and its continuous nature – because you will never 'get there': you are always in the process of becoming, not being.

An important aim of a workplace change management programme is to ensure a smooth and natural transition for staff to their new workplace. Ideally, they need to be so familiar with that new workplace that they are immediately comfortable and effective.

In business terms, this is extremely important. A reduction in productivity resulting from people feeling distracted or demotivated by change can be costly. Also, the desired benefits of the change will take longer to be realised; at worst, they may never be fully realised. It is not difficult to justify the costs of this essential investment.

To reiterate a point I touched on before, people do not like having things 'done to them' – which can include an inappropriate use of external specialists and consultants. In the case of workplace change management, it is important that ownership of the process is both internal and *perceived* to be internal. Internal change champions are invaluable.

But do also consider using external specialists who can share the workload and bring a wider perspective. Use them wisely, though – as facilitators, not managers, of change. Work with them in partnership. Don't completely hand over the process for convenience – it may well backfire on you.

As I have mentioned before, senior internal support is essential, so get senior staff involved in the programme. You will probably find that, in any case, they often have more adjustments to make than anyone else – and need more help to do so, even though they may not realise it. The point is that their involvement sends an important message to staff in terms of support and commitment to the proposed changes.

Communication

Communication is the backbone of your change management activities. Unfortunately, communication is not something we are always very good at – particularly when the messages to be delivered are difficult or complex. Use, and work with, existing resources and expertise – but be prepared to take a different approach, if appropriate.

There is a usually wide range of communication media at your disposal – so use them! Some people respond better to some media than others, so focusing on the wrong means of communication will only dilute the impact of your message.

Once you have chosen the appropriate method, make your communications stand out from the mass of other daily information. Make it exciting, stimulating and memorable: Bear in mind:

- the impact that visual media can often have over words – so use imagery, perhaps even video

- the impact that a sense of reality can bring – consider the use of models, exhibitions, and piloting

▲ the importance of two-way communication – workshops and focus groups.

And remember to keep the communication going. Regularly update staff on developments and progress. Feedback and commentary are important at all stages – but ask the right questions!

Celebrate
Finally, don't forget to celebrate success and achievement. The social aspect of the way people work and change together is important. Hold a post-move-in party! Moving into a new workplace is a good opportunity to raise morale. Many might say that we are not good at celebrating success in the workplace, so here is an opportunity to make this another of the changes you make!

staying alive

Realising, measuring and sustaining the benefits for the future

Rather than the end, this chapter represents in many ways the beginning of the journey – the new beginning ushered in, that is, by improved efficient workspace and effective working practices. The challenge is fully to realise these improvements and to ensure that you sustain them and continually adapt them to meet future challenges.

Maintenance

You need to maintain your workplace changes in two respects:

- *physically* – maintaining the functionality and appearance of the actual workspace, fixtures, fittings, technology etc

- *psychologically* – maintaining the communication and support to sustain positive attitudes, behaviours and morale.

Post-occupancy reactions

The reactions of people to a radically different workplace are varied, the degree of variance depending on the degree and quality of communication and support that you have provided.

It is not uncommon for there to be an initial 'honeymoon' period, when everything is new and exciting and staff enjoy all the attention that the new setting attracts. Then reality sets in when staff are back on their own and have to make it work. It is at this stage that old habits and 'comforts' can creep back in – so be aware of that and be prepared. At this stage some of the teething or snagging problems may also occur, and even threaten to dominate matters.

Problem-solving

We can all tend to focus on the little things that do not work at the outset, thereby overlooking the bigger success story. When this happens, don't lose heart, but be comforted by a familiar experience: after all, we take our dishwashers, central heating and cars for granted until they go wrong! However, it is important to have an effective channel for identifying and quickly remedying problems.

Building on success

It need not all be negative, though: you should provide a platform to encourage positive feedback too. You should also aim to understand how exactly you achieved your successes and how to build on them. We all need the 'feel-good' factor after a complex and challenging period of change.

To emphasise the purpose of positive feedback, call meetings 'development meetings' or set up an 'ideas board' for people to write suggestions on. Above all, if you get new ideas, try to act on them – this will give staff confidence in the process.

Aftercare

The more formal change management activities should continue too. Examples here might be:

- post-implementation workshops or focus groups

- questionnaires or interviews – to canvas views of key staff and visitors to the new workplace

- revisions of procedures etc in the light of experience

- refresher or induction training.

These activities act as a temperature gauge of how staff are feeling, and can be repeated at reasonable intervals (eg every six months) to track progress.

In some organisations, useful booklets with guidance and reference material for staff have been developed to inform and remind people about what is new. BBC Broadcast London produced such a booklet to act as an effective means of formalising and embedding their changes while also providing a cheery welcome. They ingeniously called it *The Rough Guide to Smooth Working*!

Management of the workplace

Ongoing management of the new workplace is also important. This is not just about maintaining the furniture or décor so that things look right. It is also about managing the operation of the workplace – the availability of workspace, the performance of phones and technology, the filing and storage of papers etc. It is about making sure that the agreed procedures are being followed – booking workspace, respecting others in terms of noise and adhering to those clear-desk policies.

Although the ideal is for staff to feel ownership and responsibility for all of this, a champion is often required. That may be the concierge or the office manager – or it may be you!

Realising the benefits

The purpose of aftercare is simple: to ensure that the objectives and benefits of the changes can be achieved and sustained. Such measures and objectives will of course need to have been established at the outset of the project, but it is at this stage that they become important. Measurement of benefits can be a tricky business, so it is worth exploring the topic a bit further.

Hard and soft measures

There are two types of measures involved – *hard* and *soft*. Hard measures (see opposite) are reasonably easy to quantify and convert into financial terms, but they represent only a small proportion of the real benefits of transforming your workplace. They should not be allowed to dominate your assessment.

Examples of hard measures are:

● floorplate efficiency

■ space/property savings

▲ amount of filing/storage

● occupancy costs

● individual v collaborative space

● facilities savings – eg equipment, heating

■ (reduced) cost of ongoing 'churn'

▲ ability to absorb growth/new staff

● company success (productivity/profitability)

● absenteeism.

Soft measures are less tangible and less immediate, and therefore they are more difficult to measure. Nonetheless, these are the most significant benefits that transforming your workplace can have on your business. They require trust, belief, patience and, of course, common sense.

Examples of soft measures are:

- staff motivation and productivity
- flexibility – ability to handle change
- increases in interaction and communication
- transfer of knowledge/collaboration
- visibility of leaders
- attraction and retention of staff
- image/reputation
- impact of non-action.

The last point is an interesting one. What happens if you do not make those changes to the workplace? How will productivity, competitiveness, staff retention etc be affected then?

Simple endings

There is a danger of getting too complex with all these measures. In my experience, simple anecdotes and quotations are the most powerful measures. One chief executive simply put it this way:

If everybody is happier and the company is doing better than before – it has worked!

Wouldn't it be great to have your chief executive say that about your workplace transformation project?

Finally, the workplace is no longer just a passive facility where we happen to do our business: it is a vital tool in *how* we do that business. For how much longer can you afford to ignore its potential?

I hope that this book has provided you with the advice and inspiration to think about transforming *your* workplace – and to have a go! Good luck!

appendix

Example offices

There are many excellent new office buildings that demonstrate many of the points in this book. The following are just a few of those worth looking around:

- British Airways, Waterside
- IBM, Bedfont Lakes
- BT, Stockley Park
- Rank Xerox, Marlow
- Sun Microsystems, Farnborough
- Boots, Nottingham.

There are also organisations that have achieved success within the constraints of older, existing offices. Some with which I have personally been involved include:

- Scottish Enterprise, Glasgow
- BBC Broadcast, Broadcasting House, London
- DEGW, London.

There are, of course, many more of which you may already be aware. All the examples given are normally happy to accommodate visitors, usually by appointment arranged through their facilities management team.

further reading

ADAMS S. *The Dilbert Principle*. London, Boxtree, 1997.

BECKER F. *and* STEELE F. *Workplace by Design*. San Francisco, CA, Jossey-Bass, 1995.

DUFFY F. *The New Office*. London, Conran Octopus, 1997.

VOS P., VAN MEEL J. *and* FIJCKKS A. *The Office, the Whole Office and Nothing but the Office*. Delft University of Technology, Department of Real Estate and Project Management. Available from PO Box 5043 NL 2600 Delft, the Netherlands.